LOUISIANA
ALPHABET

WRITTEN AND ILLUSTRATED BY

LAURIE PARKER

QUAIL RIDGE PRESS

"All work is meant to be heart work; it comes out of our heart and goes to the heart."

— Matthew Fox

Photographs of Louis Armstrong and Huey Long
courtesy of The Louisiana Collection,
State Library of Louisiana, Baton Rouge, Louisiana

Printed and bound in Korea by Pacifica Communications.
9 8 7 6 5 4 3 2

Library of Congress Cataloging-in-Publication Data

Parker, Laurie, 1963-
    Louisiana alphabet / written and illustrated by Laurie Parker.
       p. cm.
    ISBN 1-893062-31-7
       1. Louisiana—Juvenile literature. 2. English language—Alphabet—
Juvenile literature. [1. Louisiana—Miscellanea. 2. Alphabet.] I. Title

F369.3 .P37 2001
976.3—dc21   2001019719

QUAIL RIDGE PRESS
P. O. Box 123, Brandon, MS 39043 • 1-800-343-1583
www.quailridge.com

We love Louisiana!
So let's celebrate her!

We'll start with an

A

which is for...

ALLIGATOR!

And A is for ARMSTRONG—
none other than Louis,

AVERY ISLAND, AZALEAS, ANDOUILLE,
The town ALEXANDRIA, AUDUBON ZOO,
And AQUARIUM of the AMERICAS, too.

A's for ACADIAN, also...*Aiyee!*

That's all for A. Let's move on now to B...

ARNAUDVILLE ADDIS ABBEVILLE AMITE ANGIE

ANANDALE

ANACOCO ARCHIBALD ALTON ALLEN

Aa

ALDEN BRIDGE ALBANY

ADA

AMELIA AVONDALE ARABI ABITA SPRINGS ARCADIA

BALL   BUNKIE   BELLE CHASSE   BREAUX BRIDGE   BOUTTE

BAKER

BAWCOMVILLE

BENTON

BRIDGE CITY

Bb

BERNICE   BUCKEYE   BOURG   BALDWIN   BAPTIST

BERWICK   BROUSSARD   BAYOU CANE   BEAVER   BONFOUCA

B

Our capital seat, BATON ROUGE, starts with
And so does BALD CYPRESS—you bet! Our state tree!

B's for BOUDIN and for BISQUE and BEIGNETS,

BOURBON STREET
            BOTTOMLANDS
                        BAYOUS
                                 and BAYS.

BOGALUSA and BASTROP are both beloved places,
And so's BOSSIER CITY—a big site for races.

C

is for CAJUN—the CULTURE and food,
And there are more C words that we can include:

We have CATAHOULA, a cute spotted hound,
And old CEMETERIES
with tombs above ground.

C is for COVINGTON.
C's for CHALMETTE,
And CANE RIVER COUNTRY,
and do not forget
St. Louis CATHEDRAL,
Fine CHEFS cooking here,
And CREOLE
and CRAWFISH
and CRAB
and CHENIER!

COCODRIE   CROWLEY   CUT OFF   CARENCRO   CHAUVIN

CROZIER
CLINTON

CHACKBAY
COW ISLAND

Cc

COTTONPORT   CHENEYVILLE   COLFAX   CECILIA

CHURCH POINT   CALCASIEU   COUSHATTA   CARLYSS   COON

D

is for DELTA QUEEN—steamboat deluxe,

DENHAM SPRINGS

DEER

DRISKILL MOUNTAIN

and DUCKS.

D is for DESTREHAN,
DIXIELAND Jazz,
And, of course, DIRTY RICE.
"Dat's" a dish with pizzazz!

ERATH   ESTELLE   EASTWOOD   ELTON   ERWINVILLE

EVERGREEN

ELIZABETH

EGAN

EDGERLY

EFFIE

EXTENSION

EAST HODGE

EROS

ENGLISH TURN

EDGARD   ECHO   ESTHERWOOD   EMPIRE   EDEN ISLE

E

'S for another good eat—ÉTOUFFÉE,

And EUNICE,
where prairie land
still thrives today.

E's for EVANGELINE OAK
with its lore,

And EGRETS—
birds seen
hanging 'round by the shore.

FLOURNOY   FORDOCHE   FRENCH SETTLEMENT   FORT POLK

FRED

FLORIEN

FISHER

FAIRBANKS

FIFTH WARD

FORBING

FOLSOM

FRANKLINTON

FOREST HILL

UNION, JUSTICE & CONFIDENCE

Ff

FORKED ISLAND   FORT JESUP   FROGMORE   FARMERVILLE

F is for FILÉ, the dance FAIS-DO-DO,

And other fun FRENCH words that folks from here know.
F's for FAT TUESDAY, which we celebrate,
And Antoine "FATS" Domino, Fifties Rock great.

Some small friendly towns have an F—quite a few:
FERRIDAY

FRANKLIN

St. FRANCISVILLE, too.

And with FESTIVALS, FISHING,
our fabulous FLAG,
And world-famous FOOD—it's no wonder we brag!

G is for GUMBO
and I *GARE-ROHN-TEE*

That we've got more good things
that start with a G:
The famed GARDEN DISTRICT, with all of its style,
GRAMBLING and GRETNA, The GULF and GRAND ISLE.

There's GAMING
                    and GOSPEL
                                        and GRILLADES and GRITS,
And GALLERY—art, or a porch where one sits.

HACKBERRY   HOMER   HARVEY   HAPPY JACK   HARAHAN

HOLLY BEACH
HEAD OF ISLAND
HAYNESVILLE

HAHNVILLE
HENDERSON
HAUGHTON
HODGE

H

is for HUEY—
That's
HUEY P. LONG,

And for a rich HISTORY
that's helped make us strong.
There's Clementine HUNTER,
whose art we hold dear,
Plus Lillian HELLMAN, a playwright from here.
We've HOUMA and HAMMOND—HOMETOWNS to salute,
And HOT SAUCE and HUNTING and HOUSEBOATS to boot!

I

is for ISLANDS that dot our map's face,

And IRONWORK in railings and gates just like lace.

What is **J** for? JAMBALAYA and JAZZ,

And *JOIE DE VIVRE*—
that's Joy of Life our state has!

A key Crescent City spot's called
JACKSON SQUARE,
And J is for JENNINGS.
You must visit there!

K is for KENNER and KING CAKE and KREWE,

And K's for KISATCHIE, a lush forest, too.

L

L's for King LOUIS, the source of our name.

LA SALLE gave it to us when he staked his claim.

L is for LAKES that we have in our state,
And for plenty of things to which locals relate:

Like LEVEES, LOYOLA, our LIVE OAKS so grand,
And the pirate LAFITTE, who hid loot on our land.

L's for LAPLACE, plus LAKE CHARLES, LAFAYETTE,

And LAGNIAPPE—a little bit extra you get!

M is for MARDI GRAS—merry and bright,

And for ol' MISSISSIPPI, a river of might.
M's for some places to which you might go:
MANDEVILLE, METAIRIE, MINDEN, MONROE.

M's for MAHALIA. Who else starts with M?
The MARSALIS Family! Have you heard of them?

M's for MAGNOLIA
and MARSH
and we *gotta*

Mention a sandwich name...

mmm...
MUFFULETTA!

MORGAN CITY   MANSFIELD   MERAUX   MARINGOUIN   MIX

MATHEWS
MONTEGUT
MERRYVILLE
MANSURA

MEAUX
MOORINGSPORT
MARKSVILLE
MIDWAY

Mm

MORGANZA   MOSS BLUFF   MAMOU   MER ROUGE   MANY

NEWELLTON

NAIRN

NEGREET

NEW LLANO

NOBLE

NABORTON

NORTH HODGE

NEBO

N

N's for **NEW ORLEANS**, a place of renown,
And **NATCHITOCHES**—that is our state's oldest town.
N is for **NUTRIA** found near the water.
The name of these critters is Spanish for "otter."

O

Speaking of OTTER—it starts with an
Along with a few other things
you should know:

There's Mel OTT,
of baseball's elite Hall of Fame,
The town OPELOUSAS—
an Indian name,

OLD CAPITOL

OIL drilled OFFSHORE

OXBOW lake

And OYSTERS and OKRA
of which we partake.

P's for Brown PELICAN—it's our state bird,

And P is for PONTCHARTRAIN. What a fun word!

P's for PAUL PRUDHOMME and P's for PLANTATION.

P's for the PURCHASE from France by our nation.

P is for PARISH—a county of sorts,
And PO BOYS

and PRALINES

and PIROGUES

and PORTS!

PECAN ISLAND   PONCHATOULA   PINEVILLE   POYDRAS

PEARL RIVER

PINE PRAIRIE

PUMPKIN CENTER

POINTE A LA HACHE   PAINCOURTVILLE   PATTERSON

P p

PLAIN DEALING   PIERRE PART   PORT ALLEN   PLAQUEMINE

We've come now to **Q** Is it tricky? Well, sorta.

But here it's for French QUARTER—known as *"Da Kwaw-tah."*

R is for RUSTON and RED BEANS AND RICE,
And our RIVER ROAD route where the scenery is nice.
Anne RICE, a writer whose tales are bizarre,
And RABBITS and RIVERBOATS start with an R.
There's one other R word we really should do:
What many great recipes start with—a ROUX!

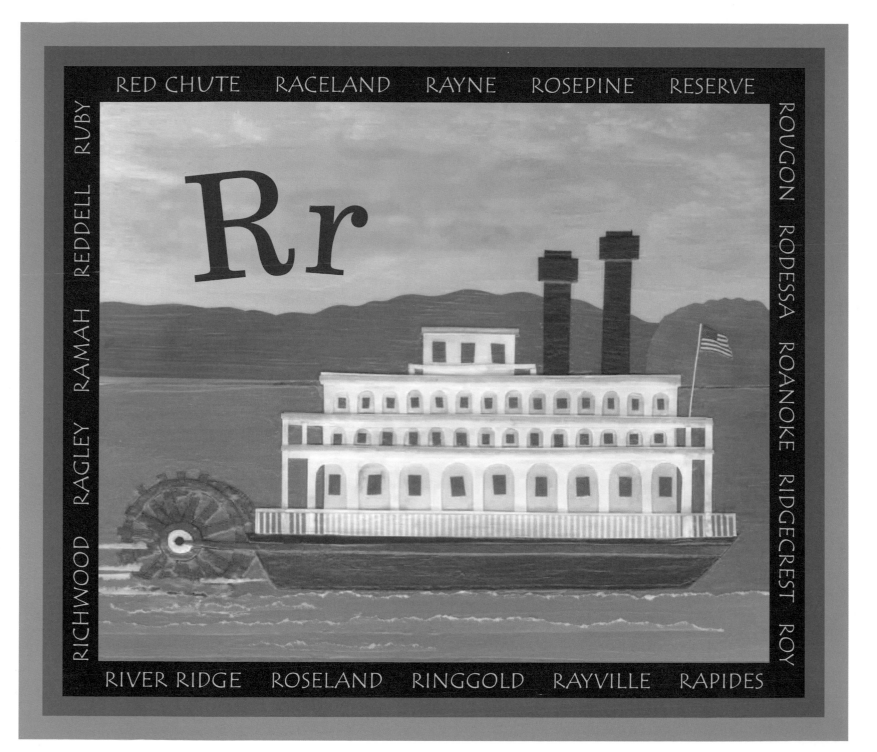

RED CHUTE   RACELAND   RAYNE   ROSEPINE   RESERVE

RUBY   REDDELL   RAMAH   RAGLEY   RICHWOOD

Rr

ROUGON   RODESSA   ROANOKE   RIDGECREST   ROY

RIVER RIDGE   ROSELAND   RINGGOLD   RAYVILLE   RAPIDES

S is for SUGAR CANE—grown as a crop,

SHRIMP, SHOTGUN HOUSES, SWAMP TOURS,
and SWAMP POP...

SPANISH MOSS, SPORTSMEN, *THE SOUTHERN REVIEW*,
The New Orleans SAINTS, and their SUPERDOME, too.

S is for some of our cities as well—
There's SHREVEPORT. There's SULPHUR. There's also SLIDELL.

S stands for STREETCAR
and one other thing:

It's "You Are My SUNSHINE,"
a song that we sing!

SWARTZ   ST. MARTINVILLE   SIMMESPORT   SUPREME   SCOTT

STARKS
SORRENTO
SIBLEY
ST. JOSEPH
START

ST. BERNARD
SAREPTA
SICILY ISLAND
SATSUMA

Ss

SPRINGHILL   ST. ROSE   SAMTOWN   SCHRIEVER   SUNSET

TIOGA   TALLULAH   TICKFAW   TERRYTOWN   TRIUMPH

TROUT   THORNWELL   TALLA BENA   TALISHEEK

TACONEY   TURKEY CREEK   TIMBERLANE   TULLOS

Tt

TREES   THERIOT   TIGERVILLE   TROPICAL BEND

T'S for the TIGERS. They're LSU's team.
And T's for TABASCO®, a hot sauce supreme!
TOLEDO BEND...THIBODAUX...
TECHE...TIMBALIER...
And TANGIPAHOA are all T words heard here.
T is for TULANE, but we are not through—
'Cause T is for TASSO and TURTLE SOUP, too!

U

UNIVERSITY starts with a U as you know,

And one we should point out is called **UNO!**

V

is for VACHERIE, VOODOO, VILLE PLATTE,
And **VENISON**, too.

Do you like to eat that?

W

We have several

words we can claim:

WETLANDS,
WISTERIA,
WOODS,
and **WILD GAME.**

X words are not often seen as a rule,
But we have XAVIER, an excellent school.

YAT. What is that? It begins with a Y.

It's a nickname that some folks in N'awlins go by.
Y'ALL know what comes next—it's the last letter, Z.
What does it stand for? Just what can it be?

It's **Z**YDECO

Music!

I bet that you guessed!

Our own unique blend,
it's a sound that has zest!

That's Louisiana — an A to Z look.
May you always have *bon temps*—

good times—with this book!